30 Quick & Easy Plant-Based Salad Recipes

A Cookbook Filled With 30 Delicious Healthy Home-Made Vegan Salad Dishes In Under 20 Minutes!

Wizard Chef

DOWNLOAD YOUR FREE GIFT NOW!

As a way of saying "thank you" for your purchase, I'm going to share with you a **Free Gift** that is exclusive to readers of "Vegan Warriors, The Meatless Spartans". This will help you to prepare your dishes easily and effortlessly without hassle!

Click Here to Check it Out

Or visit:

https://www.wizard-chef.com/wizardchefmaster

TABLE OF CONTENT

INTRODUCTION

The delicious ballad of salad

When you're up for a satiating meal ballad, it's time for a salad. Each ingredient in the salad is like a note, though mind the stringy veggies.

There's a lot of wordplay in the name as well. Hailing from Latin *salat*, meaning "salted," a salad was just a handful of leaves and herbs dunked in salty water. Those who could afford oil, vinegar, and spices created salad dressings that could even include fruits or seafood.

What was the first famous salad?

Salads were eaten since time immemorial, but two notable ones hail from 1903 and beyond.

That's when we got the Caesar Salad, comprising croutons, garlic, Parmesan cheese, boiled eggs, and olives. It was often eaten with fingers, with lettuce stems sticking out the bowl.

Another notable salad is the Aviator Salad. It too involved lettuce but also sported anchovies.

What did the first salad look like?

Think of it as the original finger food. The veggies were just torn apart, meaning there was probably a lot more chewing.

Salad ingredients were picked fresh and eaten right away. Some of those ingredients could have been nettle and dandelion before they mature.

What is the best salad veggie?

Lettuce, in all its forms, is the core salad ingredient. The ancient Egyptians started farming lettuce and set it as the norm, which soon spread to Europe.

Romans and Greeks took the idea over and spread it everywhere.

You can use any veggie in a salad, including carrots, tomatoes, radishes, colorful peppers, or mushrooms. A salad recipe is a perfect way to add new colors and aromas to one's diet.

The most popular salad greens

"Salad greens" can be any veggies, but tradition says they are the four varieties of lettuce: crisphead, romaine, looseleaf, and butterhead. Arugula, mizuna, watercress, and chicory are among other popular salad greens that can be slipped in.

Salad greens can be grown in a home garden, taking up little space but providing so much delight. They are most often eaten raw since they are delicate and bruise easily.

Can any other veggie be the salad base?

All green leafy vegetables give a lot of flavor, nutrients, and satiety with few downsides. Lettuce is the most widely grown vegetable used in a salad because of the crunch it gives. There are plenty of veggies to use in a salad, letting you experiment.

Any veggie with a variety of minerals, vitamins, and antioxidants can be the salad base. Their combined effect is lower body weight and lower blood pressure. Also, they can reduce the risk of chronic disease and prolong life.

Should one eat a salad every day?

Salad is a healthy dish for all sorts of reasons that make it the perfect dieting add-on for every health-conscious person.

A salad is made in an instant without cooking skills or cookware. One such salad fills up the tummy while giving few calories. Making and eating a salad is equally fun and healthy, helping a dieter set the diet plan straight.

Nutrients in salad greens reduce disease risks and also slow down aging.

If the veggies have some dietary fiber, the salad also regulates digestion and provides satiety.

Salads are the perfect everyday meal, with so much combo potential. A 2016 Purdue University study said a salad with one whole egg boosts the vitamin E intake by up to 600%.

Yummy vegan salads

Having a spiralizer helps make any veggie into a salad. Kale, spinach, or beets can be turned into a glorious salad in no time.

Seeds are a good idea as well. Chia, flax, or sesame seeds help give the crunch at no loss of flavor. How about a slice of avocado? Nuts work well in any salad too.

SALAD COOKBOOK

1. Lettuce, Olives, and Cherry Tomatoes Salad

Servings: 4 **Preparation Time:** 10 minutes

Nutrition Facts

Serving size: 1/4 of a recipe (6 ounces)

Percent daily values based on the Reference Daily Intake (RDI) for a 2000 calorie diet.

(Calories 74, Total Fat 4g, Total Carbohydrates 7g, Sugar 1.2g, Protein 2g)

Ingredients

½ lettuce head, finely chopped

1 lb. cherry tomatoes, halved

2 cups of olives, pitted and sliced

1 spring onion finely sliced

1 cucumber sliced

4 Tbsp. extra virgin olive oil

1 Tbsp. fresh lemon juice

Salt and freshly ground pepper to taste

Instructions

1. Mix the lettuce, tomatoes, olives, onion, and cucumber in a large salad bowl.
2. In a separate bowl, mix the oil, lemon juice, and salt and pepper to taste.
3. Drizzle olive oil mixture over salad and toss to combine well.
4. Serve.

2. Refreshing Cabbage and Carrot Salad

Servings: 4 **Preparation Time:** 10 minutes

Nutrition Facts

Serving size: 1/4 of a recipe (7.2 ounces)

Percent daily values based on the Reference Daily Intake (RDI) for a 2000 calorie diet.

(Calories 149, Total Fat 10g, Total Carbohydrates 14g, Sugar 6g, Protein 3g)

Ingredients

1 green onion finely sliced

1/2 head medium cabbage head finely chopped

1 cup of carrot grated

1/2 cup of fresh parsley chopped

4 Tbsp olive oil

2 Tbsp fresh lemon juice

Sea salt and ground pepper to taste

Instructions

1. Combine the onion, cabbage, carrot, and parsley in a large salad bowl.
2. In a small bowl, mix the olive oil with lemon juice and salt and pepper.
3. Drizzle dressing over salad and stir to combine well.
4. Serve.

3. Simple Lettuce Rainbow Salad

Servings: 4 **Preparation Time:** 10 minutes

Nutrition Facts

Serving size: 1/4 of a recipe (7 ounces)

Percent daily values based on the Reference Daily Intake (RDI) for a 2000 calorie diet.

(Calories 102, Total Fat 18g, Total Carbohydrates 15g, Sugar 3g, Protein 3g)

Ingredients

1 onion cut into rings

1 head of lettuce chopped

2 tomatoes sliced

1 large cucumber sliced

1 yellow pepper cut into strips

1/3 cup of olive oil

2 Tbs fresh lemon juice

Sea salt and ground pepper to taste

Instructions

1. Place all vegetables in a large salad bowl.
2. In a separate bowl, mix the olive oil, lemon juice, and salt, and pepper.
3. Drizzle dressing over salad and toss to combine well.
4. Serve.

4. Green Salad with Apples and Walnuts

Servings: 4 **Preparation Time:** 10 minutes

Nutrition Facts

Serving size: 1/4 of a recipe (8 ounces)

Percent daily values based on the Reference Daily Intake (RDI) for a 2000 calorie diet.

(Calories 76, Total Fat 7g, Total Carbohydrates 18g, Sugar 13g, Protein 2g)

Ingredients

1 head of green salad finely chopped (lettuce or arugula)

2 apples, cut into quarters

1/3 cup of extra-virgin olive oil

3 Tbsp lemon juice, freshly squeezed

Table salt to taste

2/3 cup of nuts chopped (almond, walnuts)

Instructions

1. Arrange the salad and apples into a large salad bowl.
2. In a small bowl, mix the remaining ingredients and sprinkle over the salad.
3. Toss to combine well and serve.

5. Arugula Salad with Champignons and Cherry Tomatoes

Servings: 4 **Preparation Time:** 10 minutes

Nutrition Facts

Serving size: 1/4 of a recipe (6 ounces)

Percent daily values based on the Reference Daily Intake (RDI) for a 2000 calorie diet.

(Calories 139, Total Fat 5g, Total Carbohydrates 7g, Sugar 2.5g, Protein 2g)

Ingredients

3 to 4 cups of arugula salad

2 cups of mushrooms sliced (champignon)

6 cherry tomatoes sliced

Dressing

4 Tbsp olive oil

2 Tbs balsamic vinegar

Salt and freshly ground white pepper to taste

Fresh basil leaves (optional)

Instructions

1. Place your salad in a large salad bowl.
2. Add the champignons and cherry tomatoes; sprinkle with a pinch of salt.
3. In a separate bowl, whisk the olive oil, vinegar and salt, and pepper to taste.
4. Drizzle dressing over salad and toss to combine well.
5. Serve.

6. Romaine Lettuce Salad with Balsamic Dressing

Servings: 4 **Preparation Time:** 15 minutes

Nutrition Facts

Serving size: 1/4 of a recipe (6 ounces)

Percent daily values based on the Reference Daily Intake (RDI) for a 2000 calorie diet.

(Calories 102, Total Fat 11g, Total Carbohydrates 22g, Sugar 14g, Protein 5g)

Ingredients

1 head of Romaine salad chopped

2 cucumbers sliced

1 onion sliced

1 shredded carrot

1/2 cup of fresh parsley finely chopped

1/3 cup of cilantro

Dressing

1/3 cup of olive oil (or avocado)

2 Tbsp balsamic vinegar

Salt and ground pepper to taste

Instructions

1. Tear the salad leaves and rinse well.
2. Place salad into a large bowl.
3. Add all remaining ingredients and gently stir.
4. In a small bowl, mix all dressing ingredients.
5. Drizzle dressing over salad and toss to combine well.
6. Serve.

7. Cabbage, Olives, and Radicchio Salad

Servings: 4 **Preparation Time:** 15 minutes

Nutrition Facts

Serving size: 1/4 of a recipe (8 ounces)

Percent daily values based on the Reference Daily Intake (RDI) for a 2000 calorie diet.

(Calories 138, Total Fat 9g, Total Carbohydrates 9g, Sugar 7g, Protein 2.5g)

Ingredients

2 cups of purple cabbage shredded (any)

2 heads of radicchio chopped

1 tomato sliced

1 cup of olives pitted

1/3 cup of extra-virgin olive oil

2 Tbsp fresh lemon juice

Salt and ground pepper to taste

Instructions

1. Clean, rinse and shred the cabbage; place in a large salad bowl.
2. Clean, rinse the radicchio, peel off the leaves one by one, and add to the salad bowl.
3. Add the cucumber and olives; gently stir.
4. In a small bowl, mix the olive oil, lemon juice, and salt and pepper to taste.
5. Drizzle evenly over salad and toss well.
6. Serve.

8. Warm Mushrooms Salad with Parsley

Servings: 4 **Preparation Time**: 15 minutes

Nutrition Facts

Serving size: 1/4 of a recipe (6.5 ounces)

Percent daily values based on the Reference Daily Intake (RDI) for a 2000 calorie diet.

(Calories 82, Total Fat 5g, Total Carbohydrates 4g, Sugar 3g, Protein 4g)

Ingredients

2 Tbs olive oil

1 small onion sliced

2 cloves garlic finely chopped

1 lb. fresh mushrooms sliced

3/4 cup of water

2 Tbs lemon juice

1/4 cup fresh parsley, chopped

2 Tbsp dill finely chopped

2 Tbsp salt and pepper to taste

Instructions

1. Heat oil in a frying pan.
2. Sauté the onion and garlic with a pinch of salt until tender.
3. Add the mushrooms, stir, cover and sauté for about 5 minutes over medium heat.
4. Transfer mushrooms into a large bowl.
5. Add the fresh parsley, dill, lemon juice, and season salt and pepper to taste.
6. Mix to combine well and serve.

9. Spicy Chinese cabbage Salad

Servings: 4 **Preparation Time**: 15 minutes

Nutrition Facts

Serving size: 1/4 of a recipe (6 ounces)

Percent daily values based on the Reference Daily Intake (RDI) for a 2000 calorie diet.

(Calories 95, Total Fat 4g, Total Carbohydrates 16g, Sugar 5g, Protein 3g)

Ingredients

2 lb. Chinese cabbage chopped

2 cloves garlic, minced

1 sweet red pepper sliced

1/2 can of corn (15.25oz)

3 Tbsp fresh parsley

2 to 3 Tbsp olive oil

1 tsp crushed paprika

Salt and ground pepper to taste

Instructions

1. Rinse and chop the Chinese cabbage; place it into a large salad bowl.
2. Add the garlic, sweet pepper, and corn; gently stir.
3. Season with paprika, salt, and pepper, and drizzle with olive oil.
4. Toss to combine well and serve.

10. Instant Brussels Sprout Salad with Mustard Dressing

Servings: 4 **Preparation Time**: 10 minutes

Nutrition Facts

Serving size: 1/4 of a recipe (8 ounces)

Percent daily values based on the Reference Daily Intake (RDI) for a 2000 calorie diet.

(Calories 113, Total Fat 1.5g, Total Carbohydrates 13g, Sugar 3g, Protein 7g)

Ingredients

1 lb. Brussels sprouts

1 cup of vegetable broth or water

Dressing

2 Tbsp vegan Dijon mustard

2 Tbsp olive oil

2 Tbsp lemon juice, freshly squeezed

1 tsp ground turmeric

Table salt and ground black pepper to taste

Instructions

1. Rinse the Brussels sprouts under cold water.
2. With a sharp knife, cut the stems and discard them.
3. Place the Instant sprouts and broth in an Instant Pot.
4. Lock lid into place and set on the MANUAL setting for 4 minutes.
5. Use the Quick release to release steam quickly.
6. Drain the Brussel sprouts into a large salad bowl.
7. In a separate bowl, mix the mustard with all remaining dressing ingredients.
8. Spread dressing over salad and toss to combine well.
9. Serve.

11. Carrot and Garlic Salad

Servings: 4 **Preparation time:** 15 minutes

Nutrition Facts

Serving size: 1/4 of a recipe (7 ounces).

Percent daily values based on the Reference Daily Intake (RDI) for a 2000 calorie diet.

(Calories 199, Total Fat 11g, Total Carbohydrates 18g, Sugar 7g, Protein 2g)

Ingredients

4 carrots grated

1 onion finely sliced

3 garlic cloves finely sliced

1/3 cup of vegetable oil (any)

1/3 cup of apple vinegar

Salt and ground pepper to taste

2 Tbsp fresh parsley finely chopped

2 Tbsp fresh chives finely chopped

Instructions

1. Grate carrots and place them in a salad bowl.
2. Add the onion and garlic.
3. In a separate bowl, mix the oil, vinegar, salt, and ground pepper.
4. Drizzle dressing over salad.
5. Sprinkle with the parsley and chives and toss to combine well.
6. Serve.

12. Broccoli Strascinati Salad (Instant Pot)

Servings: 4 **Preparation time:** 15 minutes

Nutrition Facts

Serving size: 1/4 of a recipe (7 ounces).

Percent daily values based on the Reference Daily Intake (RDI) for a 2000 calorie diet.

(Calories 148, Total Fat 10g, Total Carbohydrates 14g, Sugar 8g, Protein 2g)

Ingredients

2 lb. broccoli

2 cloves garlic crushed

2/3 cup of vegetable broth or water

1/3 cup of virgin olive oil

Salt and black ground pepper to taste

1/4 tsp ground chili pepper

Instructions

1. Clean and rinse broccoli under running water.
2. Place the broccoli, broth, and garlic in Instant Pot.
3. Lock lid into place and set on the MANUAL setting for 8 minutes.
4. Use a Quick release and rinse the broccoli.
5. Place broccoli in a salad bowl, and season with salt, pepper, chili pepper, and oil.
6. Serve immediately.

13. Spring Mixed Salad

Servings: 4

Preparation time: 15 minutes

Nutrition Facts

Serving size: 1/4 of a recipe (6.5 ounces)

Percent daily values based on the Reference Daily Intake (RDI) for a 2000 calorie diet.

(Calories 89, Total Fat 8g, Total Carbohydrates 16g, Sugar 7g, Protein 2g)

Ingredients

1 head of lettuce finely chopped

1 bunch of fresh celery finely chopped

1 large cucumber sliced

1 onion sliced

1 tomato sliced

1 carrot grated

1 radish thinly sliced

1/2 cup of extra-virgin olive oil to taste

2 Tbsp apple vinegar

Salt and ground pepper to taste

Instructions

1. Prepare the lettuce and all vegetables and arrange them into a salad bowl.
2. In a separate bowl, mix the oil, vinegar, and salt, and pepper.
3. Drizzle your salad with the oil mixture and gently stir to combine well.
4. Serve.

14. Sun-dried Tomatoes and Lettuce Salad

Servings: 4 **Preparation time:** 10 minutes

Nutrition Facts

Serving size: 1/4 of a recipe (6.5 ounces).

Percent daily values based on the Reference Daily Intake (RDI) for a 2000 calorie diet.

(Calories 101, Total Fat 15g, Total Carbohydrates 8g, Sugar 7g, Protein 1g)

Ingredients

1 cup of sun-dried tomatoes in oil chopped (drained)

1 head of lettuce salad chopped

1 small onion finely sliced

3 Tbsp extra virgin olive oil

salt to taste

A headful of fresh chopped basil (optional)

Instructions

1. Arrange the lettuce and place the sun-dried tomatoes.
2. Add the onion slices and season with salt to taste.
3. Drizzle with olive oil, and sprinkle with fresh basil.
4. Serve.

15. Pico de Gallo - Mexican Salad

Servings: 3 **Preparation time:** 10 minutes

Nutrition Facts

Serving size: 1/4 of a recipe (6 ounces).

Percent daily values based on the Reference Daily Intake (RDI) for a 2000 calorie diet.

(Calories 125, Total Fat 6g, Total Carbohydrates 11g, Sugar 9g, Protein 2g)

Ingredients

3 tomatoes cut into small cubes

1 large onion chopped

4 Tbsp fresh coriander finely chopped

1 chili pepper slices

1 fresh lime juice (from 1 lime)

2 Tbsp olive oil

Salt to taste

Tortillas for serving

Instructions

1. Cut the tomatoes into cubes and put them in a salad bowl.
2. Add the onion, coriander, chili pepper.
3. Sprinkle with lime juice, olive oil, and season with salt to taste.
4. Serve with tortillas.

16. Quinoa Tabouleh Salad

Servings: 3 **Preparation time:** 15 to 17 minutes

Nutrition Facts

Serving size: 1/4 of a recipe (6 ounces).

Percent daily values based on the Reference Daily Intake (RDI) for a 2000 calorie diet.

(Calories 197, Total Fat 10g, Total Carbohydrates 21g, Sugar 4g, Protein 6g)

Ingredients

1 cup of quinoa

3 cups of water

3 spring onions finely chopped

1 tomato cut into small cubes

1/3 cup of fresh mint finely chopped

1/3 cup of fresh parsley, finely chopped

salt and ground pepper to taste

3 Tbsp olive oil

Fresh lemon juice (from 1 lemon)

lemon slices for serving

Instructions

1. Rinse the quinoa under running water.
2. Cook for about 12 minutes over medium heat.
3. Strain your quinoa and place it in a salad bowl.
4. Add the onion, tomato, mint, parsley and gently stir.
5. Season with salt and pepper to taste.
6. Drizzle with olive oil and lemon juice
7. Serve with lemon slices.

17. Warm Chicory Greens and Beets Salad

Servings: 2 to 3 **Preparation time:** 15 to 17 minutes

Nutrition Facts

Serving size: 1/4 of a recipe (6 ounces)

Percent daily values based on the Reference Daily Intake (RDI) for a 2000 calorie diet.

(Calories 316, Total Fat 19g, Total Carbohydrates 23g, Sugar 17g, Protein 40

Ingredients

1 lb. chicory greens (or kale)

2 cups of beets sliced, cooked

salt and ground pepper to taste

3 Tbsp olive oil

balsamic vinegar to taste

2 tbsp cumin seeds

Instructions

1. Clean and rinse the chicory greens (or kale) with plenty of water.
2. Boil your greens for about 12 to 13 minutes.
3. Remove from the heat, strain, and cool with water.
4. Place the greens in a large salad bowl.
5. Add sliced beets, and season with salt and pepper.
6. Sprinkle with the olive oil and balsamic vinegar; gently stir.
7. Finally, sprinkle with cumin, and serve.

18. Savoy Cabbage and Potato Salad (Instant Pot)

Servings: 4 **Preparation Time:** 20 minutes

Nutrition Facts

Serving size: 1/4 of a recipe (8 ounces)

Percent daily values based on the Reference Daily Intake (RDI) for a 2000 calorie diet.

(Calories 298, Total Fat 3g, Total Carbohydrates 57g, Sugar 3g, Protein 11g)

Ingredients

1 1/2 lb. potatoes peeled and cut into cubes

1 cup of vegetarian broth or water

4 cups of fresh savoy cabbage finely chopped

4 Tbsp fresh parsley finely chopped

1 Tbsp fresh celery chopped

Salt and ground pepper to taste

2 Tbsp olive or avocado oil

Instructions

1. Place the potatoes and the broth or water in an Instant pot.
2. Lock lid into place and set on the MANUAL setting for 10 minutes.
3. Use the Natural Release and carefully open the lid.
4. Rinse your potatoes and place in a large salad bowl; mash with a fork.
5. Add the Savoy cabbage, parsley, and celery; gently stir.
6. Drizzle with oil and season the salt and pepper to taste.
7. Serve.

19. Bibb Lettuce Salad with Sweet Lemon Vinaigrette

Servings: 4 **Preparation Time:** 15 minutes

Nutrition Facts

Serving size: 1/4 of a recipe (7 ounces).

Percent daily values based on the Reference Daily Intake (RDI) for a 2000 calorie diet.

(Calories 232, Total Fat 19g, Total Carbohydrates 10g, Sugar 6g, Protein 3g)

Ingredients

Salad

8 cups of bibb lettuce salad chopped

2 tomatoes finely sliced

1 large carrot finely sliced

Vinaigrette

1/3 cup of olive oil

Fresh lemon juice from 2 lemons

2 tsp granulated sugar

Salt and ground pepper to taste

Instructions

1. Place the bib lettuce salad, tomatoes, and carrots in a salad bowl.
2. In a separate bowl, mix the oil, lemon juice, and sugar.
3. Drizzle the vinaigrette over salad and toss to combine well.
4. Serve immediately.

20. Lollo Rosso Salad with Peas

Servings: 3 **Preparation Time:** 10 minutes

Nutrition Facts

Serving size: 1/3 of a recipe (6 ounces).

Percent daily values based on the Reference Daily Intake (RDI) for a 2000 calorie diet.

(Calories 87, Total Fat 4g, Total Carbohydrates 14g, Sugar 6g, Protein 8g)

Ingredients

1 lb. Lollo Rosso salad chopped

1 green onion finely sliced

1 cup of peas (canned)

3 Tbsp olive oil

Fresh lemon juice (from 1 lemon)

Salt and ground pepper to taste

Instructions

1. Rinse and chop the salad and place it into a large salad bowl.
2. Add the green onion and peas.
3. Season with olive oil, lemon juice, and salt and pepper to taste.
4. Serve.

21. Loose-leaf Lettuce Salad with Tofu

Servings: 4 **Preparation Time:** 15 minutes

Nutrition Facts

Serving size: 1/4 of a recipe (7.5 ounces).

Percent daily values based on the Reference Daily Intake (RDI) for a 2000 calorie diet.

(Calories 107, Total Fat 11g, Total Carbohydrates 10g, Sugar 3g, Protein 6g)

Ingredients

1 head of Loose-leaf lettuce

1 onion sliced

1 greenhorn pepper sliced

1 large cucumber sliced

4 cherry tomatoes halved

1 cup of olives, pitted

1/2 cup of Tofu, firm and cut into small cubes

4 Tbsp olive oil

2 Tbs fresh lemon juice

Salt and pepper to taste

Instructions

1. Cut off the looseleaf lettuce outer leaves and finely chop; rinse.
2. Place the salad into a large salad bowl.
3. Add all remaining ingredients and gently stir.
4. Season with salt and pepper to taste.
5. Sprinkle with olive oil and lemon juice; toss.
6. Serve.

22. Salad with Cauliflower Rice, Pines, and Cranberries

Servings: 4 to 5 **Preparation Time**: 10 minutes

Nutrition Facts

Serving size: 1/4 of a recipe (8 ounces).

Percent daily values based on the Reference Daily Intake (RDI) for a 2000 calorie diet.

(Calories 153, Total Fat 9g, Total Carbohydrates 12g, Sugar 7g, Protein 5g)

Ingredients

1 cauliflower cut into florets

2 spring onions finely sliced

2 clove garlic minced

1 chili pepper sliced

3 Tbsp ground almonds

1 Tbsp pines

2 Tbsp olive oil

1 Tbsp fresh lemon juice (1 lemon)

4 Tbsp cranberries, dried

1 Tbsp cumin

Fresh mint finely chopped (to taste)

Salt to taste

Mustard for serving (optional)

Instructions

1. Cut the cauliflower into small florets and remove the stalk.
2. Put the cauliflower in the food processor and ground it.
3. Boil the cauliflower rice for about 5 minutes with a little salt, rinse.
4. Place the spring onions, garlic, pepper, and cauliflower rice in a big salad bowl.
5. Season salad with salt to taste and gently mix.
6. Add all remaining ingredients, toss.
7. Serve with mustard (optional).

23. Creamy Chickpeas, Avocado and Coriander Salad

Servings: 4

Preparation Time: 10 minutes

Nutrition Facts

Serving size: 1/4 of a recipe (6 ounces).

Percent daily values based on the Reference Daily Intake (RDI) for a 2000 calorie diet.

(Calories 160, Total Fat 10g, Total Carbohydrates 9g, Sugar 1g, Protein 5g)

Ingredients

1 cup of chickpeas (canned)

1 avocado cut into cubes

lemon juice and zest from 1 lemon

1/2 cup of fresh coriander, finely chopped

4 Tbsp fresh mint finely chopped

1 clove garlic, finely chopped

3 Tbsp olive oil

1 Tbsp cumin

Salt and ground pepper to taste

1/2 cup of water (optional)

Instructions

1. Place all ingredients in a fast-speed blender or a food processor.
2. Beat or process until smooth and creamy.
3. If your salad is too thick, add little water.
4. Taste and adjust seasonings.
5. Keep refrigerated.

24. Broccoli with Cranberries and Hazelnuts Salad

Servings: 4 **Preparation Time:** 10 minutes

Nutrition Facts

Serving size: 1/4 of a recipe (6 ounces).

Percent daily values based on the Reference Daily Intake (RDI) for a 2000 calorie diet.

(Calories 136, Total Fat 5g, Total Carbohydrates 11g, Sugar 9g, Protein 5g)

Ingredients

1 lb. broccoli cut into florets

1 red onion sliced

1/2 cup of cranberries

1/2 cup of hazelnuts sliced

Dressing

4 Tbsp Extra-virgin olive oil

1 Tbsp Dijon mustard

1 Tbsp fresh lemon juice

Salt and freshly ground black pepper to taste

Instructions

1. Heat water in a saucepan and boil broccoli for about 7 minutes; drain.
2. Place the broccoli florets in a large salad bowl.
3. Add the cranberries and hazelnuts.
4. Mix the oil, mustard, lemon juice, and salt and pepper to taste in a separate bowl.
5. Drizzle dressing over salad and gently stir.
6. Serve.

25. Zucchini Salad with Sour - Sweet Soy Dressing

Servings: 4 **Preparation Time:** 10 minutes

Nutrition Facts

Serving size: 1/4 of a recipe (7 ounces).

Percent daily values based on the Reference Daily Intake (RDI) for a 2000 calorie diet.

(Calories 108, Total Fat 6g, Total Carbohydrates 9g, Sugar 8g, Protein 3g)

Ingredients

4 zucchinis sliced

2 onions sliced

1 red pepper sliced

Dressing

2 Tbsp sesame oil (or olive)

1/3 cup of rice vinegar (or apple cider vinegar)

2 tsp strained honey

1/3 cup of soy sauce

sesame seeds for serving

Instructions

1. Slice your zucchini and place it in a large salad bowl.
2. Add the onions and red pepper.
3. In a separate bowl, mix all dressing ingredients.
4. Pour dressing over salad and stir well.
5. Serve.

26. Colorful Cabbage, Avocado, and Quinoa Salad

Servings: 4 **Preparation Time:** 15 minutes

Nutrition Facts

Serving size: 1/4 of a recipe (8 ounces).

Percent daily values based on the Reference Daily Intake (RDI) for a 2000 calorie diet.

(Calories 138, Total Fat 2g, Total Carbohydrates 22g, Sugar 1g, Protein 10g)

Ingredients

1/4 head of red cabbage shredded

1 onion finely chopped

1 avocado cut into cubes

1 cup of mushrooms sliced

5 cherry tomatoes sliced

1 cup of quinoa (cooked)

2 Tbsp fresh chives chopped

1 Tbsp fresh cilantro chopped

2 tablespoons olive oil

Lemon juice to taste

Salt to taste

Instructions

1. Place quinoa in an Instant Pot and add one cup of water.
2. Lock lid in a place and press the "MANUAL" button; cook for 1 minute on high pressure.
3. Use the quick release, and carefully open the lid.
4. Rinse the quinoa under running water; drain and set aside.
5. Place the cabbage, onion, avocado, and mushrooms in a large salad bowl.
6. Add the cherry tomatoes and quinoa, and sprinkle with a pinch of salt; stir.
7. Drizzle with the oil and lemon juice and toss to combine well.
8. Taste and adjust the salt.
9. Serve.

27. Asian Protein Salad

Servings: 3 **Preparation Time:** 15 minutes

Nutrition Facts

Serving size: 1/3 of a recipe (7 ounces)

Percent daily values based on the Reference Daily Intake (RDI) for a 2000 calorie diet.

(Calories 201, Total Fat 4g, Total Carbohydrates 27g, Sugar 8g, Protein 22g)

Ingredients

A handful of fresh watercress chopped

A handful of fresh arugula chopped

A handful of the baby - spinach

1 cup of pumpkin cubes (canned)

4 Tbsp chickpeas (canned)

1 Tbsp pumpkin seeds

1 Tbsp Flax seeds

3 Tbsp Soy sauce

2 Tbsp extra virgin olive oil

1 Tbsp Sesame oil

Instructions

1. Combine the watercress, arugula, and spinach in a salad bowl; mix well.
2. Add the pumpkin, chickpeas, pumpkin seeds, and flax seeds.
3. In a separate bowl, mix the Soy sauce, olive oil, and sesame oil.
4. Drizzle over salad and gently stir.
5. Serve.

28. Cucumber and Radish Salad with Cumin and Cashew

Servings: 3 **Preparation Time:** 15 minutes

Nutrition Facts

Serving size: 1/3 of a recipe (7.3 ounces).

Percent daily values based on the Reference Daily Intake (RDI) for a 2000 calorie diet.

(Calories 229, Total Fat 8g, Total Carbohydrates 24g, Sugar 6g, Protein 17g)

Ingredients

2 cucumbers sliced

1 bunch of small radishes, trimmed and cut in four

1 green pepper, seeded, cut into strips

1/2 tablespoon of mustard seeds

1 tablespoon of cumin seeds

1/2 cup of toasted cashew nuts, finely chopped

1/4 cup coriander leaves chopped

4 Tbsp olive oil

2 Tbsp fresh lemon juice

Salt and pepper to taste

Instructions

1. Place the cucumbers and radishes in a salad bowl.
2. Sprinkle with a bit of salt.
3. Add the green pepper, mustard seeds, cumin seeds, coriander, and cashew.
4. In a separate bowl, mix the oil, lemon juice, and salt, and pepper.
5. Drizzle over salad and stir to combine well.
6. Serve.

29. Vegan Caesar Salad

Servings: 2 to 3

Preparation Time: 15 minutes

Nutrition Facts

Serving size: 1/3 of a recipe (7.3 ounces).

Percent daily values based on the Reference Daily Intake (RDI) for a 2000 calorie diet.

(Calories 234, Total Fat 38g, Total Carbohydrates 9g, Sugar 3g, Protein 5g)

Ingredients

1 large head of Romaine lettuce

1 cup of soft Tofu cut into cubes

1 cup of croutons

1/2 cup of olive oil

1/4 cup of fresh lemon juice

1 tsp Dijon mustard

1 Tbsp nutritional yeast

salt and black pepper to taste

Instructions

1. Rinse and chop your salad into bite-sized pieces; place into a large salad bowl.
2. Add the tofu cheese and croutons.
3. In a separate bowl, whisk the olive oil, lemon juice, mustard, yeast, and salt and pepper.
4. Drizzle the mixture over salad and toss to combine well.
5. Serve.

30. Tropical Lettuce Salad

Servings: 4 **Preparation Time:** 10 minutes

Nutrition Facts

Serving size: 1/4 of a recipe (7 ounces)

Percent daily values based on the Reference Daily Intake (RDI) for a 2000 calorie diet.

(Calories 158, Total Fat 9g, Total Carbohydrates 11g, Sugar 8g, Protein 3g)

Ingredients

1/2 head of lettuce salad

a bunch of arugula leaves

2 tangerines cut into pieces (or fresh peach)

1 small red onion cut into slices

4 Tbsp olive oil

1 Tbsp balsamic vinegar

2 Tbsp pineapple juice (or peach)

salt to taste

Instructions

1. Arrange the lettuce and arugula onto the salad bowl.
2. Add the tangerines and onion over the salad.
3. In a separate bowl, mix the oil, vinegar, juice, and salt to taste.
4. Drizzle the mixture over the salad.
5. Serve.

Conclusion

Salads are a splendid way to make the dinner table much more appealing. They are tasty, light, and simple to make.

Whether you are dieting or not, do give salads a try and you too can write your salad ballad.

It is important to eat a variety of fresh fruits and vegetables, in as many different colors as possible. Combining them in a salad is both easy and delicious! Loaded with vitamins and minerals, eating a salad a day will also increase the level of powerful antioxidants in your blood.

Sources:

- https://foodal.com/knowledge/paleo/9-good-reasons-to-eat-a-salad-a-day/
- https://medlineplus.gov/ency/article/002132.htm
- https://betterme.world/articles/salad-and-water-diet/
- https://www.verywellfit.com/the-best-salad-ingredients-to-lose-weight-3495220
- https://www.everydayhealth.com/healthy-recipes/healthy-salad-dos-and-donts.aspx
- https://www.lra.org/uploads/1/0/6/5/106519639/ch_4_pp_pt_2.ppt

Congrats! Note from the Wizard Chef

You've reached the end of the book!

Thank you for finishing 30 Quick & Easy Plant-Based Salad Recipes: A Cookbook Filled With 30 Delicious Healthy Home-Made Vegan Salad Dishes In Under 20 Minutes!

If so, would you mind taking 30 seconds to leave a quick review on Amazon? We worked hard to bring you books that you enjoy! Plus, it helps authors like us produce more books like this in the future!

Here's where to go to leave a review now:

=> *http://successwithnow.com/30-plantbased-salads*

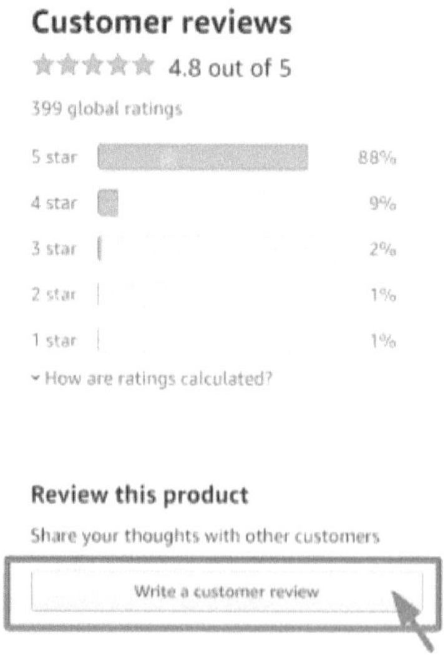

Customer reviews

4.8 out of 5

399 global ratings

5 star 88%

4 star 9%

3 star 2%

2 star 1%

1 star 1%

How are ratings calculated?

Review this product

Share your thoughts with other customers

Write a customer review

www.ingramcontent.com/pod-product-compliance
Ingram Content Group UK Ltd.
Pitfield, Milton Keynes, MK11 3LW, UK
UKHW041642190726
13854UKWH00006B/2653